Consistent Profits: Maximizing Gains Trading Related Stocks

Harmony Weaver

Copyright © 2024 by Harmony Weaver All rights reserved. No part of this publication may be reproduced, distributed, or transmitted in any form or by any means, including photocopying, recording, or other electronic or mechanical methods, without the prior written permission of the publisher, except in the case of brief quotations embodied in critical reviews and certain other noncommercial uses permitted by copyright law.

Disclaimer: 7
Introduction: 9
Chapter 1: Understanding Sympathy Moves 12
Chapter 2: Identifying Sympathy Plays 40
Chapter 3: Case Studies of Successful Sympathy Plays. 57
Chapter 4: Strategy Development 77
Chapter 5: Executing Sympathy Plays 95
Chapter 6: Common Pitfalls and How to Avoid Them 103
Chapter 7: Advanced Techniques and Insights 114
Chapter 8: Building a Community and Continuous Learning 123
Conclusion: 132
Bonus Template and Checklist 138

Disclaimer:

The information provided in this book is for educational and informational purposes only. The content is not intended as, and should not be construed to be, financial, investment, tax, legal, or any other kind of professional advice. Readers are encouraged to seek professional advice tailored to their individual circumstances before making any investment decisions.

Investing in the stock market involves risk, including the possible loss of principal. Past performance is not indicative of future results. While the author has made every effort to ensure the accuracy of the information contained in this book, there is no guarantee that the strategies discussed will be successful or that readers will achieve any specific results.

The author and publisher disclaim any liability, loss, or risk incurred directly or indirectly from the use or application of any information contained in this book. Readers should conduct their own research and due diligence and consult with a qualified financial advisor before making any investment decisions.

By reading this book, you acknowledge that you understand and agree to these terms.

Introduction:

Welcome to "Consistent Profits: Maximizing Gains Trading Related Stocks." If you've ever found yourself overwhelmed by the complexities of stock trading, you're not alone. The market can seem like an intricate web of numbers, trends, and strategies, often leaving even seasoned investors perplexed. However, through my research and experience, I've discovered a phenomenon that simplifies the process and offers a straightforward path to consistent gains: sympathy moves.

Sympathy moves, or sympathy plays, occur when a significant price change in one stock triggers similar movements in related stocks within the same sector or industry. This ripple effect happens because investors anticipate that the factors driving the initial stock's performance will likely impact its peers. Understanding and leveraging this phenomenon can provide a clear and effective strategy for making profitable trades.

In this book, we will examine the mechanics of sympathy moves, exploring why they happen, how to identify them, and the best ways to profit from them. You don't need to be an expert in technical analysis or have an advanced degree in finance to benefit from this strategy. By focusing on sector relationships and market psychology, sympathy moves offer an accessible and reliable approach to stock investing.

Based on my extensive research, I believe sympathy plays represent one of the easiest ways to gain an advantage in the stock market. Unlike other strategies that require constant monitoring of charts and patterns, sympathy moves rely on observing broader market trends and sector dynamics. This makes it possible for everyday investors to capitalize on these opportunities without needing to spend countless hours analyzing data.

Throughout this book, I will share practical insights, real-world examples, and step-by-step strategies to help you master sympathy trading. We will look at historical case studies to understand how successful sympathy plays have unfolded in the past and discuss how you can spot similar opportunities in today's market.

Whether you're a novice investor looking to get started or a seasoned trader seeking to refine your strategy, this book will provide you with the knowledge and tools to make sympathy moves a core part of your investment approach. By the end of this journey, you'll be equipped to identify and act on sympathy plays with confidence, unlocking consistent profits in the stock market.

So, let's dive in and explore how sympathy moves can transform your trading strategy and bring you closer to achieving your financial goals.

Chapter 1: Understanding Sympathy Moves

What are Sympathy Moves?

Sympathy moves, also known as sympathy plays, refer to the phenomenon where the price movement of one stock influences the price movement of related stocks. This often occurs within the same sector or industry, but can also extend to companies with similar business models or those facing the same economic conditions. For instance, if a leading technology company reports excellent quarterly earnings, it's common to see a rise in the stock prices of other technology companies as well. This occurs because investors anticipate that positive news for one company might imply similar success for its peers.

Sympathy moves are driven by market psychology and the behavior of investors who seek to capitalize on perceived opportunities. When a company within a specific sector experiences a significant event, such as a positive earnings report, a product launch, or a regulatory approval, investors may assume that related companies will benefit from the same favorable conditions. This assumption leads to increased buying activity across the sector, driving up the prices of related stocks.

Why Do Sympathy Moves Occur?
To understand why sympathy moves occur, it's essential to be aware of the psychology of investors and the interconnected nature of markets. Here are some key reasons:

Market Sentiment:
Market sentiment plays a crucial role in sympathy moves. When investors feel optimistic about a particular company's prospects, this sentiment can spread to other companies in the same sector. For example, if a pharmaceutical company announces a breakthrough drug

approval, investors may become more optimistic about other pharmaceutical companies, leading to a sector-wide rally.

Sector Correlation:
Stocks within the same sector or industry tend to move together because they are often affected by the same external factors, such as economic conditions, regulatory changes, and technological advancements. Positive news for one company can imply favorable conditions for the entire sector, prompting investors to buy shares in related companies.

Investor Herding:
Herding behavior, where investors follow the actions of others, can amplify sympathy moves. When investors see others buying stocks in a particular sector following positive news, they may join in, driving up prices even further. This collective behavior can create a self-reinforcing cycle, leading to significant price movements across related stocks.

Algorithmic Trading:
In today's markets, algorithmic trading plays a substantial role in sympathy moves. Algorithms programmed to identify correlations between stocks can quickly execute trades based on news events, amplifying price movements across related stocks. These algorithms can react faster than human traders, contributing to rapid and significant sympathy moves.

Historical Examples of Sympathy Moves
Examining historical examples can provide a clearer understanding of how sympathy moves unfold and their impact on the market. Let's look at a few notable instances:

Tesla and Electric Vehicle Stocks
Tesla, a leading electric vehicle (EV) manufacturer, has often influenced the stock prices of other EV companies. For example, when Tesla reported record deliveries and earnings in early 2021, the stock prices of other EV

manufacturers like NIO, Xpeng, and Li Auto also surged. Investors believed that Tesla's success signaled strong demand for electric vehicles, benefiting the entire sector.

Apple and Technology Stocks
Apple's influence on technology stocks is well-documented. When Apple announces new products or reports strong financial results, it often boosts the stock prices of its suppliers and competitors. For instance, when Apple launched the iPhone 12 with 5G capabilities, companies involved in 5G technology and Apple's supply chain, such as Qualcomm and Broadcom, saw their stock prices rise due to anticipated increased demand for their products.

Pfizer and Pharmaceutical Stocks
During the COVID-19 pandemic, Pfizer's announcement of a successful vaccine trial in November 2020 had a profound impact on the stock market. Not only did Pfizer's stock soar, but other pharmaceutical companies involved in

vaccine development, like Moderna and BioNTech, also experienced significant gains. Investors believed that the success of one vaccine would pave the way for others, leading to a sector-wide rally.

Meme Stocks: GameStop, AMC, and Heavily Shorted Stocks
One of the most remarkable examples of sympathy moves in recent history involves the meme stock phenomenon, particularly the cases of GameStop (GME) and AMC Entertainment (AMC). These stocks became central figures in a unique market event driven by retail investors from online communities, most notably Reddit's WallStreetBets. The catalyst for these sympathy moves was not traditional financial news but a concerted effort by retail investors to counteract heavy short positions held by institutional investors.

The GameStop Surge

In January 2021, GameStop's stock price experienced an unprecedented surge. The company, which was heavily shorted by hedge funds, became the focus of a massive buying campaign by retail investors. The aim was to create a short squeeze, where rising stock prices force short sellers to buy back shares at higher prices to cover their positions, further driving up the stock price.

As GameStop's stock price skyrocketed, it created a wave of enthusiasm and attention. Retail investors, emboldened by their success, started looking for other heavily shorted stocks that could be targeted in a similar manner.

AMC Entertainment and Other Heavily Shorted Stocks
AMC Entertainment became another prime target. Like GameStop, AMC was also heavily shorted, and retail investors saw an opportunity to replicate the short squeeze. As a result, AMC's

stock price soared, drawing in more investors and generating significant media coverage.

The impact didn't stop with AMC. Investors began scanning the market for other heavily shorted stocks, leading to sympathy moves in a range of companies. Stocks like Bed Bath & Beyond (BBBY), BlackBerry (BB), and Nokia (NOK) also saw substantial price increases as they were caught up in the wave of retail investor enthusiasm.

Mechanics Behind the Meme Stock Sympathy Moves
The meme stock phenomenon highlighted several key aspects of sympathy moves:

Heavy Short Interest:
The initial trigger for these sympathy moves was the high level of short interest in GameStop and AMC. Retail investors identified these stocks as prime candidates for a short squeeze, leading to coordinated buying efforts.

Social Media Influence:
Social media platforms, particularly Reddit, played a crucial role in amplifying these moves. The collective action and sentiment shared on these platforms created a powerful force that drove stock prices higher.

Investor Herding and FOMO:
The fear of missing out (FOMO) drove many investors to join the rally. As GameStop and AMC surged, more investors piled in, hoping to catch the wave, which in turn pushed the stock prices even higher.

Algorithmic and Institutional Response:
The rapid price movements and high trading volumes attracted the attention of algorithmic trading systems and institutional investors. This added another layer of buying activity, further amplifying the sympathy moves.

Lessons from Meme Stock Sympathy Moves

The meme stock phenomenon offers several important lessons for understanding and capitalizing on sympathy moves:

Identifying Key Triggers:
While traditional sympathy moves often follow positive news or earnings reports, the meme stock example shows that social dynamics and market sentiment can also be powerful triggers. Monitoring social media and online forums can provide early indicators of potential sympathy moves.

Understanding Market Psychology:
The meme stock surge was driven by a combination of short interest, social media influence, and investor psychology. Recognizing these factors can help investors identify similar opportunities in the future.

Managing Risks:
Meme stocks demonstrated the importance of managing risks. While the potential for quick

gains was significant, the volatility and unpredictability of these stocks also posed substantial risks. Having a clear risk management strategy is essential when participating in sympathy moves.

Leveraging Technology:
The role of algorithmic trading in amplifying meme stock moves highlights the importance of technology in modern trading. Utilizing advanced trading tools and analytics can provide an edge in identifying and capitalizing on sympathy plays.

Conclusion
Sympathy moves present a powerful strategy for capitalizing on sector-wide trends and investor sentiment. Whether driven by traditional news events or unique phenomena like meme stocks, understanding the mechanics and psychology behind these moves is crucial for success. By staying informed, analyzing market reactions, and implementing effective trading strategies,

investors can harness the potential of sympathy moves to achieve consistent gains in the stock market.

Differentiating Sympathy Moves from Other Market Phenomena
Sympathy moves are distinct from other market phenomena, such as correlation, contagion, and co-movement. While these terms are often used interchangeably, they have specific meanings in the context of financial markets:

Correlation:
Correlation refers to the statistical relationship between two variables. In the stock market, it measures how two stocks move in relation to each other. While correlated stocks may move together, correlation alone does not explain the underlying reasons for these movements. Sympathy moves, on the other hand, are driven by investor behavior and sentiment.

Contagion:

Contagion describes the spread of market disturbances from one region or market to another. It often occurs during financial crises when negative events in one market trigger panic selling in other markets. Sympathy moves can be seen as a form of contagion, but they are typically driven by positive news rather than negative events.

Co-Movement:
Co-movement refers to the tendency of assets to move together over time. This can be due to shared economic factors, market sentiment, or sector-specific news. Sympathy moves are a specific type of co-movement triggered by news events affecting a particular company or sector.

Understanding these distinctions helps clarify why sympathy moves occur and how they differ from other market behaviors. This knowledge is crucial for developing effective trading strategies based on sympathy plays.

The Mechanics of Sympathy Moves

To effectively capitalize on sympathy moves, it's important to understand the mechanics behind them. Here's a step-by-step look at how sympathy moves typically unfold:

Trigger Event:

A significant news event, such as an earnings report, product launch, regulatory approval, or major announcement, serves as the trigger for sympathy moves. This event generates attention and interest among investors.

Initial Stock Reaction:

The stock directly affected by the news event experiences a rapid price movement. This could be an upward surge following positive news or a sharp decline following negative news.

Investor Interpretation:

Investors interpret the news event and consider its implications for other companies in the same sector or industry. Positive news for one company may lead investors to believe that other companies will benefit similarly, while negative news may have the opposite effect.

Sector-Wide Impact:
As investors buy or sell stocks based on their interpretations, related stocks in the same sector begin to move in sympathy. This creates a sector-wide impact, with multiple stocks experiencing similar price movements.

Algorithmic Amplification:
Algorithmic trading systems, programmed to detect correlations and react to news events, can amplify sympathy moves. These systems execute trades quickly, further driving price movements across related stocks.

Sustained Momentum:
If the news event has long-term implications, sympathy moves can sustain momentum over several days or weeks. Investors continue to

adjust their positions based on evolving market sentiment and additional information.

Identifying Sympathy Plays

Successfully identifying sympathy plays requires a combination of market awareness, sector knowledge, and timely execution. Here are some key steps to help you spot potential sympathy moves:

Stay Informed:
Keep abreast of news and developments in the sectors you're interested in. Follow industry-specific news sources, company announcements, and economic indicators that could impact stock prices.

Monitor Key Players:
Identify the key players in each sector and understand their relationships. Knowing which companies are leaders, suppliers, competitors, or partners can help you anticipate how news events might impact related stocks.

Analyze Market Reactions:
Study how stocks have reacted to past news events. Analyzing historical data can provide insights into typical sympathy moves and help you develop a sense of how the market responds to different types of news.

Use Screening Tools:
Utilize stock screening tools to identify potential sympathy plays. These tools can help you filter stocks based on sector, market capitalization, trading volume, and recent price movements.

Watch for Early Signals:
Look for early signals of sympathy moves, such as pre-market trading activity or unusual trading volumes. These signals can indicate that investors are starting to react to news events, providing an opportunity to act early.

Leverage Social Media and Forums:

Social media platforms and online forums can be valuable sources of real-time information and sentiment analysis. Following discussions and trending topics can help you stay ahead of the curve and identify emerging sympathy plays.

Practical Example: Sympathy Moves in Action
To illustrate how sympathy moves work in real-time, let's consider a detailed example involving a breakthrough announcement by Company A, a leading semiconductor manufacturer, and its impact on other companies within the same sector.

The Trigger Event
Company A has been working on a groundbreaking chip technology that promises to significantly enhance performance while reducing manufacturing costs. After months of research and development, Company A announces that its new chip has passed all regulatory hurdles and is ready for mass production. This news is released after the

market closes, creating a buzz among investors and industry analysts.

After-Hours Trading
Immediately following the announcement, Company A's stock price begins to surge in after-hours trading. Investors who are quick to react recognize the potential impact of this breakthrough on Company A's market position and future earnings. The excitement and optimism drive a sharp increase in the stock price, as investors scramble to buy shares before the market officially opens the next day.

Market Open
When the market opens the following day, the momentum continues. The strong after-hours performance leads to a gap-up at the market open, with Company A's stock opening significantly higher than its previous closing price. The buying frenzy intensifies as more investors become aware of the news, and those

who missed the after-hours trading rush to get in on the action.

Sector Reaction

As the news spreads, investors begin to consider the broader implications for the semiconductor sector. They realize that Company A's breakthrough will likely have a positive impact on other companies in the industry as well. Here's how:

Suppliers and Partners:
Company A relies on several suppliers for raw materials and components. Companies B and C, which supply essential parts to Company A, are expected to benefit from increased orders. Investors anticipate higher revenues for these suppliers as Company A ramps up production.

Competitors:
Company D, a direct competitor to Company A, may also see a positive impact. While initially it might seem counterintuitive, the breakthrough

could validate the demand for advanced semiconductor technology, lifting the entire market. Investors might speculate that Company D will step up its innovation efforts, leading to potential future gains.

Complementary Businesses:
Companies E and F, which manufacture complementary technologies or devices that use semiconductors, could see increased demand for their products. As Company A's new chip technology becomes more widely adopted, the need for compatible products might rise, benefiting these companies.

Sympathy Moves
With these considerations in mind, investors start to buy shares of Companies B, C, D, E, and F. The increased buying activity drives up the stock prices of these related companies, creating a wave of sympathy moves across the sector. Let's break down this process step-by-step:

Company B and C (Suppliers):
Investors anticipate that Company A's ramp-up in production will lead to higher demand for components from its suppliers. As a result, the stock prices of Companies B and C start to rise, reflecting the expected increase in their sales and revenues.

Company D (Competitor):
Although initially perceived as a competitor, Company D's stock benefits from the overall positive sentiment in the semiconductor sector. Investors believe that the technological breakthrough will drive innovation and growth across the industry, leading to a rise in Company D's stock price.

Companies E and F (Complementary Businesses):
As investors predict increased adoption of Company A's new chip technology, they also foresee higher demand for devices and technologies that incorporate these chips.

Consequently, the stock prices of Companies E and F, which produce such devices, begin to climb.

Algorithmic Trading
In today's fast-paced markets, algorithmic trading systems play a significant role in amplifying sympathy moves. These systems are programmed to detect correlations and react to news events almost instantaneously. Here's how they come into play:

News Detection:
Algorithmic trading systems scan news sources and financial reports for keywords and significant announcements. When Company A's breakthrough news is released, these systems quickly identify it as a major event.

Correlation Analysis:
The algorithms analyze historical data to determine which stocks have shown a correlation with Company A in the past. They

identify Companies B, C, D, E, and F as related stocks based on their historical price movements and industry relationships.

Trade Execution:
Once the correlations are established, the algorithms execute trades in these related stocks. They buy shares of Companies B, C, D, E, and F, anticipating that these stocks will move in sympathy with Company A. The rapid execution of these trades further drives up the stock prices of the related companies.

Sustained Rally
If the news has long-term implications, the sympathy moves can sustain momentum over several days or even weeks. Here's how the scenario might unfold:

Continued Buying Activity:
As more investors learn about Company A's breakthrough and its potential impact on the sector, they continue to buy shares of related

stocks. This sustained buying activity helps maintain the upward momentum in the stock prices of Companies B, C, D, E, and F.

Positive Earnings Reports:
In the following quarters, as Company A's new chip technology starts generating revenue, Companies B and C report higher earnings due to increased orders. These positive earnings reports further validate the initial investor optimism, driving additional gains in their stock prices.

Industry Growth:
The semiconductor industry as a whole benefits from the increased demand for advanced technology. As companies in the sector invest in innovation and expand their production capacities, the entire industry experiences growth. This broader industry growth supports sustained price increases in related stocks.

Long-Term Investments:

Institutional investors and mutual funds, recognizing the long-term potential of the semiconductor sector, start to allocate more capital to these stocks. Their large-scale investments provide additional support for the sustained rally.

Risk Management and Considerations
While sympathy moves offer significant profit opportunities, they also come with risks. It's important to manage these risks effectively:

Overreactions:
Sometimes, the initial enthusiasm can lead to overreactions, with stock prices rising too quickly and becoming overvalued. Investors should be cautious and avoid getting caught in the hype without solid fundamental analysis.

Diversification:
To mitigate risks, it's essential to diversify investments across different sectors and industries. Relying solely on sympathy moves

within one sector can expose investors to sector-specific risks.

Monitoring News Flow:
Continuously monitor news and developments related to the sector. Changes in market conditions, regulatory environments, or new technological advancements can impact the sustainability of sympathy moves.

Profit-Taking Strategy:
Implement a profit-taking strategy to lock in gains. Setting target prices and stop-loss orders can help manage risk and ensure that profits are realized before any potential reversal in stock prices.

Conclusion
Sympathy moves present a powerful strategy for capitalizing on sector-wide trends and investor sentiment. By understanding the mechanics behind these moves and identifying potential opportunities, investors can position themselves

for consistent gains in the stock market. The key lies in staying informed, analyzing market reactions, and executing trades with a clear strategy in mind.

In the next chapter, we will go further into the process of identifying sympathy plays, including tools and techniques to spot these opportunities before they unfold. With a solid understanding of how sympathy moves work and a strategic approach to trading, you can unlock the potential for consistent profits in the stock market.

Chapter 2: Identifying Sympathy Plays

Sector Relationships and Connections
Understanding sector relationships and connections is fundamental to identifying sympathy plays. Stocks within the same sector often move in tandem because they are influenced by similar economic, regulatory, and market conditions. This interconnection makes it possible to predict the movement of related stocks when a significant event impacts one stock in the sector.

Industry Classification:
Stocks are grouped into sectors and industries based on their primary business activities. Common classification systems include the Global Industry Classification Standard (GICS) and the Industry Classification Benchmark (ICB). Familiarity with these classifications helps in

understanding which stocks are likely to be related.

Supply Chain Relationships:
Companies within the same supply chain often exhibit correlated stock movements. For example, if a major automotive manufacturer reports strong sales, its suppliers of parts and raw materials may also see their stock prices rise. Understanding the upstream and downstream connections within an industry can help identify potential sympathy plays.

Competitive Landscape:
Competitors within the same sector are likely to be influenced by the same market trends and news events. Positive news for one company can signal good prospects for its competitors, leading to a rise in their stock prices as well. Conversely, negative news can have a similar, albeit inverse, effect.

Geographical Factors:

Companies operating in the same geographical region may face similar economic conditions, regulatory environments, and market trends. These factors can create a correlation in their stock movements. For instance, technology companies based in Silicon Valley might experience similar impacts from regional policy changes or local economic trends.

Industry and Sector Dynamics
To effectively identify sympathy plays, it's crucial to understand the dynamics of different industries and sectors. Each sector has unique characteristics and drivers that influence stock movements.

Technology Sector:
The technology sector is driven by innovation, product launches, and market adoption of new technologies. News about technological breakthroughs, regulatory approvals, or significant product releases can trigger sympathy moves among tech stocks. For

example, when a leading tech company announces a new smartphone, related stocks in the semiconductor, software, and hardware sectors may also rise.

Healthcare Sector:
The healthcare sector is heavily influenced by regulatory decisions, drug approvals, and healthcare policies. Positive clinical trial results or FDA approvals for one pharmaceutical company can lead to sympathy moves in related biotech and pharmaceutical stocks. Additionally, changes in healthcare regulations or government funding can impact the entire sector.

Energy Sector:
The energy sector is affected by geopolitical events, changes in commodity prices, and environmental regulations. A rise in oil prices due to geopolitical tensions can lead to sympathy moves in oil and gas exploration companies, refining businesses, and energy

equipment manufacturers. Similarly, news about renewable energy initiatives can boost stocks of companies involved in solar, wind, and other renewable energy sources.

Financial Sector:
The financial sector is influenced by interest rates, economic data, and regulatory changes. Positive earnings reports from major banks can trigger sympathy moves in other financial stocks, including investment firms, insurance companies, and regional banks. Conversely, changes in interest rates set by central banks can have wide-reaching effects on the sector.

Consumer Discretionary Sector:
The consumer discretionary sector, which includes retail, automotive, and leisure companies, is driven by consumer spending trends and economic indicators. Strong retail sales data or positive consumer confidence reports can lead to sympathy moves across the sector. Additionally, seasonal factors, such as

holiday shopping periods, can influence stock movements.

Identifying Related Stocks

Identifying related stocks is a key step in capitalizing on sympathy plays. Here are some strategies to help pinpoint stocks that are likely to move together:

Peer Analysis:
Conduct a peer analysis to identify companies that operate in the same industry and share similar market conditions. Tools like industry reports, financial news, and stock screeners can help identify peers. For example, within the EV sector, companies like Tesla, NIO, and Rivian can be considered peers.

Supplier and Customer Analysis:
Analyze the supply chain relationships to identify stocks that may be impacted by news affecting a key player in the chain. For instance, if a major retailer reports strong sales, its

suppliers and logistics providers might also benefit, creating potential sympathy plays.

ETF Holdings:
Exchange-traded funds (ETFs) often hold a basket of related stocks within a specific sector or industry. Reviewing the holdings of sector-specific ETFs can provide insights into related stocks that may be influenced by sector-wide news.

Correlation Analysis:
Utilize statistical tools to analyze historical correlations between stocks. Stocks with high positive correlations are more likely to exhibit sympathy moves. Financial websites and trading platforms often provide correlation matrices and analysis tools to help identify these relationships.

News and Earnings Reports:
Monitor news and earnings reports for leading companies in a sector. The impact on these companies can provide clues about potential

sympathy moves in related stocks. For example, earnings beats or misses from industry leaders can set the tone for the sector.

Economic Indicators and Catalysts
Economic indicators and catalysts play a significant role in triggering sympathy moves. Understanding these factors can help you anticipate potential market reactions.

Economic Data Releases:
Key economic data releases, such as GDP growth, unemployment rates, inflation figures, and consumer spending reports, can influence entire sectors. For example, strong GDP growth might boost the consumer discretionary sector, leading to sympathy moves in retail and automotive stocks.

Interest Rate Decisions:
Central bank decisions on interest rates can have broad implications for financial markets. A rate hike might benefit financial stocks due to higher

lending margins, while a rate cut could boost consumer spending and benefit retail stocks. Monitoring central bank announcements can provide early signals for sympathy plays.

Regulatory Changes:
Regulatory changes and government policies can significantly impact certain sectors. For instance, new environmental regulations might favor renewable energy stocks while negatively affecting traditional energy companies. Keeping track of legislative developments and policy changes is crucial for identifying potential sympathy moves.

Geopolitical Events:
Geopolitical events, such as trade agreements, conflicts, and diplomatic developments, can create market volatility and influence related stocks. For example, a trade agreement between two countries might boost stocks in export-oriented sectors, while geopolitical tensions could impact defense stocks.

Corporate Events:
Corporate events, such as mergers and acquisitions, product launches, and management changes, can act as catalysts for sympathy moves. A major acquisition in the tech sector might lead to increased interest in other tech stocks, while a high-profile product launch could boost related companies in the supply chain.

Key Indicators to Watch
To successfully identify and capitalize on sympathy plays, it's important to monitor key indicators that signal potential market movements:

Trading Volume:
Unusual trading volume can indicate increased investor interest and potential sympathy moves. Spikes in volume often precede significant price movements, providing early entry opportunities.

Price Action:
Analyzing price action, such as breakouts, gaps, and trends, can help identify stocks poised for sympathy moves. Technical analysis tools, like moving averages and trend lines, can provide additional insights.

Options Activity:
Monitoring options activity, such as unusual options volume or significant changes in open interest, can provide clues about investor sentiment and potential sympathy plays. High options activity often indicates that investors are positioning for a major move.

Short Interest:
High short interest in a stock can amplify sympathy moves, especially if positive news triggers a short squeeze. Monitoring short interest data can help identify stocks with the potential for significant price movements.

Insider Trading:

Insider trading activity, such as purchases or sales by company executives, can signal confidence or concern about future prospects. Insider buying often precedes positive price movements, making it a valuable indicator for potential sympathy plays.

Common Triggers for Sympathy Moves
Identifying common triggers for sympathy moves can enhance your ability to predict and capitalize on these opportunities:

Earnings Reports:
Positive or negative earnings reports from a leading company in a sector can trigger sympathy moves in related stocks. Strong earnings often signal favorable conditions for the sector, while weak earnings can have the opposite effect.

Product Launches:
Major product launches, especially in technology and consumer goods sectors, can influence

related stocks. The success of a new product can boost supplier stocks and competitors as well.

Regulatory Approvals:
Regulatory approvals, such as drug approvals in the healthcare sector or environmental permits in the energy sector, can trigger sympathy moves. These approvals often indicate favorable prospects for related companies.

Macroeconomic Announcements:
Macroeconomic announcements, such as changes in interest rates, inflation data, and employment reports, can impact entire sectors. For example, a rate cut might boost consumer spending and benefit retail stocks.

Geopolitical Events:
Geopolitical events, such as trade deals, conflicts, and policy changes, can create market volatility and trigger sympathy moves. Trade agreements, for instance, can benefit export-oriented sectors.

Industry Conferences:
Industry conferences and trade shows often serve as platforms for major announcements and product showcases. Positive news emerging from these events can trigger sympathy moves across the sector.

Analyst Upgrades/Downgrades:
Analyst upgrades or downgrades for leading companies can influence investor sentiment and trigger sympathy moves. Positive analyst reports often lead to increased buying activity in related stocks.

Practical Steps to Identify Sympathy Plays
To effectively identify sympathy plays, follow these practical steps:

Stay Informed:
Regularly monitor news sources, financial reports, and industry publications to stay updated on sector developments. Use financial

news websites, subscription services, and social media platforms to gather real-time information.

Utilize Screening Tools:
Use stock screening tools to filter stocks based on sector, industry, trading volume, and other criteria. Many trading platforms offer customizable screeners to help identify potential sympathy plays.

Conduct Peer Analysis:
Perform peer analysis to identify related stocks within a sector. Compare financial metrics, performance trends, and market positioning to identify stocks that are likely to move in sympathy.

Monitor Economic Indicators:
Keep an eye on economic indicators and macroeconomic data releases. Understand how these indicators impact different sectors and use this information to anticipate sympathy moves.

Analyze Technical Patterns:
Utilize technical analysis to identify price patterns, trends, and key support/resistance levels. Look for technical signals that indicate potential sympathy moves, such as breakouts or trend reversals.

Watch Options Activity:
Monitor options activity for unusual volume or changes in open interest. Options activity can provide early signals of investor sentiment and potential sympathy moves.

Track Insider Trading:
Keep track of insider trading activity to gauge insider confidence or concern about future prospects. Insider buying can be a strong indicator of potential positive price movements.

By combining these strategies and tools, you can effectively identify and capitalize on sympathy plays. The next chapter will delve into executing trades based on sympathy plays, including timing, risk management, and strategies for maximizing profits. With a comprehensive approach to identifying sympathy plays, you can enhance your trading success and achieve consistent gains in the stock market.

Chapter 3: Case Studies of Successful Sympathy Plays

Historical Case Studies

Understanding sympathy plays through historical case studies provides valuable insights into how these market phenomena unfold. By examining successful examples, we can identify patterns, strategies, and key lessons that can be applied to future trading opportunities.

Case Study 1: The Dot-Com Boom (1999-2000)
Background:
The late 1990s saw an explosion in internet and technology stocks, collectively known as the dot-com boom. Companies associated with the internet, regardless of their profitability or business models, experienced massive stock price increases. Key players like Amazon, Yahoo, and eBay became household names and industry leaders.

Trigger Event:
Amazon's IPO in 1997 marked a significant milestone. As Amazon's stock price soared, it drew attention to the potential of internet-based companies. This enthusiasm quickly spread to other tech stocks.

Sympathy Moves:

Yahoo: Benefited significantly as investors sought exposure to the internet sector. Yahoo's stock price soared as it became a leading web portal and search engine.

eBay: Another major beneficiary, eBay's stock surged following Amazon's success, driven by investor optimism about online commerce.

Lessons Learned:

Sector Enthusiasm: When a key player in a sector performs exceptionally well, it often sparks enthusiasm for the entire sector.

Investor Sentiment: Positive sentiment can drive substantial sympathy moves, even in companies with less established business models.

Bubble Dynamics: It's crucial to recognize the potential for speculative bubbles, as excessive enthusiasm can lead to unsustainable stock prices.

Case Study 2: The Housing Market Crisis (2007-2008)

Background:

The financial crisis of 2007-2008 was triggered by the collapse of the housing market, leading to widespread financial turmoil. Key players in the mortgage and financial sectors experienced significant stock price declines.

Trigger Event:

The collapse of Lehman Brothers in September 2008 was a major event. Lehman's bankruptcy signaled the severity of the crisis, leading to panic across the financial sector.

Sympathy Moves:

Goldman Sachs: Although more resilient, Goldman Sachs experienced substantial stock price declines due to its exposure to mortgage-backed securities and the overall market panic.

Bank of America: Faced severe losses as investors feared further financial sector instability. Its stock price dropped sharply in sympathy with Lehman Brothers.

Lessons Learned:

Negative Sympathies: Sympathy moves can be both positive and negative. Negative news in a key player can lead to widespread declines in related stocks.

Systemic Risk: Understanding systemic risks is crucial, as issues in one company can quickly spread across an entire sector.

Importance of Diversification: Diversification helps mitigate risk during sector-wide downturns triggered by negative sympathy moves.

Case Study 3: The Rise of FAANG Stocks (2010s)

Background:
The FAANG stocks (Facebook, Apple, Amazon, Netflix, and Google) became dominant forces in the technology sector throughout the 2010s. Their growth and success had profound impacts on the tech industry and the broader market.

Trigger Event:
Apple's consistent innovation and market leadership, particularly with the iPhone, set the stage. Each new product release often led to significant stock price increases for Apple.

Sympathy Moves:

Facebook: Benefited from Apple's success by association. As the tech sector thrived, Facebook's advertising business grew, leading to substantial stock price increases.

Netflix: Also saw sympathy moves as streaming and digital entertainment gained popularity, partly driven by broader tech adoption and Apple's ecosystem growth.

Lessons Learned:

Sector Leadership: Leading companies can drive sympathy moves across their sectors, boosting related stocks.

Innovation and Growth: Continuous innovation by key players creates positive sentiment for the entire sector.

Long-Term Trends: Sympathy moves can extend over longer periods, especially in rapidly growing sectors like technology.

Detailed Analysis of Successful Examples

Example 1: Tesla and the Electric Vehicle (EV) Boom

Background:

Tesla has been a pioneer in the electric vehicle market. Its success has had a ripple effect on other EV manufacturers and related companies.

Trigger Event:

In 2020, Tesla reported record deliveries and achieved consistent profitability, leading to its inclusion in the S&P 500 index. This milestone significantly boosted investor confidence.

Sympathy Moves:

NIO: A Chinese EV manufacturer, saw its stock price surge as investors looked for other EV opportunities following Tesla's success.
Xpeng: Another Chinese EV company, experienced similar gains, driven by positive sentiment in the EV sector.
Analysis:

Sector Expansion: Tesla's success highlighted the potential of the EV market, leading to increased investment in related stocks.
Investor Optimism: Positive news about Tesla's growth and profitability fueled optimism for other EV manufacturers.

Global Impact: The sympathy moves extended globally, benefiting EV companies in different regions.

Lessons Learned:

Market Leadership: The success of a leading company can have a global impact on related stocks.

Growth Potential: Investors seek opportunities in sectors with high growth potential, leading to significant sympathy moves.

Cross-Border Influence: Sympathy plays can transcend national boundaries, influencing stocks worldwide.

Example 2: GameStop and the Meme Stock Phenomenon

Background:

The meme stock phenomenon in early 2021 saw a surge in the stock prices of heavily shorted companies, driven by retail investors on platforms like Reddit's WallStreetBets.

Trigger Event:

GameStop became the focal point as retail investors targeted it for a short squeeze. The stock price skyrocketed from around $20 to over $400 in a matter of weeks.

Sympathy Moves:

AMC Entertainment: Also heavily shorted, AMC's stock surged as retail investors extended their efforts to other companies.

BlackBerry: Another target, BlackBerry's stock price increased significantly due to its high short interest and the momentum from GameStop.

Analysis:

Short Interest Focus: High short interest made these stocks attractive targets for retail investors looking to trigger short squeezes.

Social Media Coordination: Platforms like Reddit played a crucial role in coordinating buying efforts and driving sympathy moves.

Market Volatility: The rapid price increases led to heightened market volatility and significant trading volume.

Lessons Learned:

Retail Investor Power: Retail investors can drive substantial sympathy moves, especially with coordinated efforts.

Short Squeeze Dynamics: High short interest stocks are particularly susceptible to dramatic price movements.

Social Media Influence: Social media platforms can amplify sympathy moves and create new market dynamics.

Lessons Learned from Each Case

Analyzing these historical examples provides several key lessons:

Market Sentiment: Positive or negative sentiment can drive sympathy moves across sectors. Understanding market psychology is crucial.

Sector Leadership: Leading companies have a significant influence on related stocks. Monitoring their performance and news can provide early signals.

High Short Interest: Stocks with high short interest are susceptible to dramatic sympathy moves, especially in volatile market conditions.

Innovation and Growth: Sectors characterized by innovation and high growth potential are more likely to experience sustained sympathy moves.

Systemic Risk: Negative news can trigger widespread declines, highlighting the importance of diversification and risk management.

Analyzing Recent Examples

Recent Example 1: The COVID-19 Vaccine Race

Background:

The race to develop COVID-19 vaccines in 2020 had significant impacts on pharmaceutical and biotech stocks.

Trigger Event:

Pfizer and BioNTech's announcement of a successful vaccine trial in November 2020 marked a major milestone. The news led to a sharp increase in their stock prices.

Sympathy Moves:

Moderna: Another leading vaccine developer, saw its stock price surge following positive news from Pfizer and BioNTech.
AstraZeneca: Experienced similar gains as investors anticipated success across multiple vaccine developers.
Analysis:

Sector-Wide Impact: Positive news for one vaccine developer boosted confidence in the entire sector.
Global Health Crisis: The urgent need for vaccines created significant investor interest and market volatility.

Collaborative Efforts: Partnerships and collaborations among companies amplified the sympathy moves.

Lessons Learned:

Global Events: Major global events, like the COVID-19 pandemic, can drive sympathy moves across sectors.

Collaborative Success: Success in collaborative efforts can lead to sector-wide optimism and investment.

Market Volatility: High-stakes scenarios create significant market volatility and trading opportunities.

Recent Example 2: Cryptocurrency and Blockchain Stocks

Background:

The rise of cryptocurrencies and blockchain technology has created new investment opportunities and driven sympathy moves in related stocks.

Trigger Event:

Bitcoin's surge in 2020 and 2021, reaching new all-time highs, drew significant investor interest in cryptocurrencies and blockchain technology.

Sympathy Moves:

Riot Blockchain: A company involved in cryptocurrency mining, saw its stock price rise in sympathy with Bitcoin's gains.
Marathon Digital Holdings: Another cryptocurrency mining company, experienced similar increases due to the overall enthusiasm for cryptocurrencies.
Analysis:

Sector Correlation: The performance of Bitcoin and other cryptocurrencies directly influenced related stocks.
Investor Speculation: High investor interest and speculation drove substantial sympathy moves in the sector.

Technological Innovation: The potential of blockchain technology created long-term growth prospects for related companies.
Lessons Learned:

Emerging Technologies: Emerging technologies can create new investment opportunities and significant sympathy moves.
Market Speculation: High levels of speculation can drive rapid price movements and volatility.
Correlation with Assets: The performance of related assets, like cryptocurrencies, can significantly impact stock prices.
Current Market Examples and Their Outcomes
Example 1: Renewable Energy Sector
Background:
The renewable energy sector has gained significant attention due to increasing environmental concerns and government policies promoting clean energy.

Current Trigger Event:

Government initiatives and subsidies for renewable energy projects have boosted investor confidence.

Sympathy Moves:

First Solar: A leading solar panel manufacturer, has seen its stock price rise due to positive sentiment in the renewable energy sector.
Enphase Energy: A company specializing in solar energy solutions, has experienced similar gains driven by sector-wide optimism.
Outcomes:

Long-Term Growth: The renewable energy sector is expected to see sustained growth due to environmental policies and technological advancements.
Investment Influx: Increased investment in clean energy projects has driven stock prices and created new opportunities for investors.
Practical Insights:

Policy Influence: Government policies and subsidies can significantly impact sector performance and create sympathy moves.
Sustained Trends: Long-term trends, such as the shift towards renewable energy, provide ongoing investment opportunities.

Example 2: Artificial Intelligence (AI) and Automation

Background:
The AI and automation sector is experiencing rapid growth due to advancements in technology and increasing adoption across industries.

Current Trigger Event:
Major advancements in AI technologies and significant investments by leading tech companies have driven investor interest.

Sympathy Moves:

NVIDIA: Known for its AI hardware and software solutions, has seen its stock price rise due to the growing demand for AI technologies.

C3.ai: A company specializing in enterprise AI solutions, experienced similar gains driven by sector-wide enthusiasm.

Outcomes:

Technological Leadership: Companies leading in AI innovation are likely to drive sympathy moves across the sector.

Investment Opportunities: The increasing adoption of AI and automation creates significant investment opportunities and potential for growth.

Practical Insights:

Technological Advancements: Staying informed about technological advancements can help identify early investment opportunities.

Sector Enthusiasm: High investor enthusiasm for emerging technologies can drive substantial sympathy moves.

Practical Insights and Takeaways

Analyzing historical and recent case studies of successful sympathy plays provides valuable practical insights:

Monitor Leading Companies: Keeping an eye on leading companies within a sector can provide early signals for sympathy moves. Positive news and performance from these companies often influence related stocks.

Understand Sector Dynamics: Each sector has unique characteristics and drivers. Understanding these dynamics helps identify potential sympathy plays and anticipate market reactions.

Leverage Economic Indicators: Economic indicators and macroeconomic data releases can significantly impact sectors. Monitoring these indicators helps anticipate sympathy moves and market trends.

Utilize Technical Analysis: Technical analysis tools, such as price patterns and volume indicators, can provide early signals of potential sympathy moves.

Stay Informed: Regularly monitor financial news, industry reports, and market developments to stay updated on potential triggers for sympathy plays.

Diversify Investments: Diversification helps mitigate risk and capitalize on multiple sympathy plays across different sectors.

Adapt to Market Conditions: Market conditions and investor sentiment can change rapidly. Being adaptable and responsive to new information is crucial for successful trading.

By applying these practical insights and strategies, traders and investors can effectively identify and capitalize on sympathy plays, enhancing their potential for consistent gains in the stock market.

Chapter 4: Strategy Development

Developing a robust strategy for identifying and capitalizing on sympathy plays is crucial for consistent success in stock market investing. This chapter will guide you through the process of creating a sympathy play strategy, including step-by-step instructions, essential tools and resources, risk management techniques, and strategies for diversification and hedging.

Creating a Sympathy Play Strategy
A well-defined strategy is the foundation of successful trading. By systematically approaching sympathy plays, you can maximize your potential for profits while minimizing risks.

Step 1: Define Your Objectives
Clarify Your Goals:

Start by defining your investment goals. Are you looking for short-term gains, long-term growth, or a combination of both? Understanding your objectives will shape your strategy and risk tolerance.

Set Performance Targets:
Establish clear performance targets, such as a specific percentage return on investment or a set dollar amount. These targets will help you measure the success of your strategy and make necessary adjustments.

Step 2: Conduct Sector and Industry Analysis
Identify Potential Sectors:
Conduct thorough research to identify sectors with high potential for sympathy plays. Look for sectors that are experiencing significant developments, such as technological advancements, regulatory changes, or economic shifts.

Analyze Key Players:

Within each sector, identify the leading companies and understand their market influence. Analyze their financial health, growth prospects, and historical stock performance. Leading companies often drive sympathy moves across their sectors.

Understand Sector Dynamics:
Study the unique characteristics and dynamics of each sector. Understand the supply chain relationships, competitive landscape, and key economic indicators that influence the sector. This knowledge will help you anticipate potential sympathy plays.

Step 3: Monitor News and Market Events
Stay Informed:
Regularly monitor financial news, industry reports, and market developments. Subscribe to reputable financial news sources, follow industry experts on social media, and join investment forums to stay updated on potential triggers for sympathy plays.

Track Earnings Reports:
Pay close attention to earnings reports from leading companies. Positive or negative earnings can trigger significant sympathy moves in related stocks. Use financial calendars to track upcoming earnings announcements.

Watch for Economic Indicators:
Monitor key economic indicators, such as GDP growth, inflation rates, and employment data. These indicators can influence entire sectors and trigger sympathy moves. Understanding their impact on the market will help you anticipate potential opportunities.

Step 4: Identify Related Stocks
Conduct Peer Analysis:
Identify companies within the same sector that are likely to be influenced by the performance of leading companies. Use financial tools and stock screeners to find peers based on market

capitalization, revenue, and industry classification.

Analyze Correlations:
Utilize statistical tools to analyze historical correlations between stocks. Stocks with high positive correlations are more likely to exhibit sympathy moves. Financial websites and trading platforms often provide correlation matrices and analysis tools.

Evaluate Supply Chain Relationships:
Understand the supply chain relationships within a sector. Identify key suppliers, customers, and partners of leading companies. News affecting one company can create ripple effects across its supply chain, leading to potential sympathy plays.

Step 5: Develop Entry and Exit Strategies
Set Entry Criteria:
Define clear criteria for entering a trade. Consider factors such as stock price movements,

trading volume, and technical indicators. Entry criteria should be based on objective data to minimize emotional decision-making.

Establish Exit Points:
Determine exit points for each trade. Set profit targets and stop-loss levels to protect your investments. Exit points should be based on realistic expectations and risk tolerance.

Use Technical Analysis:
Incorporate technical analysis tools, such as moving averages, trend lines, and support/resistance levels, to refine your entry and exit strategies. Technical analysis can help you identify optimal trading opportunities and minimize risks.

Step 6: Implement Risk Management Techniques
Diversify Your Portfolio:
Diversification helps spread risk across multiple investments. Allocate your capital across

different sectors and industries to reduce exposure to any single stock or market event.

Utilize Stop-Loss Orders:
Use stop-loss orders to limit potential losses. A stop-loss order automatically sells a stock when it reaches a predetermined price, helping you manage risk and protect your investments.

Regularly Review and Adjust:
Regularly review your strategy and adjust it based on market conditions and performance. Stay flexible and be willing to make changes as needed to improve your strategy and achieve your investment goals.

Tools and Resources Needed
To develop and execute a successful sympathy play strategy, you need access to various tools and resources. Here are some essential ones:

Financial News Sources
Reputable Financial News Websites:

Websites like Bloomberg, Reuters, CNBC, and MarketWatch provide up-to-date financial news, market analysis, and industry reports.

Industry Publications:
Subscribe to industry-specific publications and newsletters. These sources offer in-depth analysis and insights into specific sectors.

Stock Screeners and Analysis Tools

Stock Screening Platforms:
Use stock screening platforms like Finviz, TradeStation, and Zacks to filter stocks based on various criteria, such as sector, industry, market capitalization, and financial metrics.

Technical Analysis Tools:
Platforms like TradingView and MetaTrader offer advanced technical analysis tools, including charting capabilities, technical indicators, and pattern recognition.

Economic and Financial Data

Economic Calendars:
Track key economic data releases and events using economic calendars provided by websites like Investing.com and Forex Factory.

Financial Data Providers:
Access comprehensive financial data and market information through providers like Bloomberg Terminal, FactSet, and Yahoo Finance.

Trading Platforms

Online Brokers:
Choose a reliable online broker that offers a robust trading platform, low fees, and access to a wide range of stocks and financial instruments. Popular brokers include TD Ameritrade, E*TRADE, and Interactive Brokers.

Mobile Trading Apps:
Utilize mobile trading apps to monitor your investments and execute trades on the go. Many brokers offer mobile apps with advanced features and real-time data.

Risk Management

Effective risk management is crucial for long-term success in stock market investing. By assessing and mitigating risks, you can protect your investments and enhance your potential for profits.

Assessing Risks

Identify Potential Risks:
Evaluate the potential risks associated with each trade, including market volatility, economic events, and company-specific factors. Understanding these risks helps you make informed decisions and manage your investments effectively.

Measure Risk Tolerance:
Determine your risk tolerance based on your investment goals, time horizon, and financial situation. Assessing your risk tolerance helps you set appropriate risk management strategies and avoid emotional decision-making.

Analyze Historical Data:
Review historical data and past performance of stocks to identify patterns and potential risks. Historical analysis provides valuable insights into how stocks and sectors react to various market conditions.

Mitigating Risks

Diversification:
Diversify your portfolio across different sectors, industries, and asset classes to spread risk and reduce exposure to any single investment. Diversification helps protect your portfolio from sector-specific downturns.

Hedging Techniques:
Utilize hedging techniques to protect your investments from potential losses. Common hedging strategies include options trading, inverse ETFs, and futures contracts.

Implement Stop-Loss Orders:

Set stop-loss orders for each trade to limit potential losses. Stop-loss orders automatically sell a stock when it reaches a predetermined price, helping you manage risk and protect your investments.

Regularly Review and Adjust:
Regularly review your portfolio and adjust your investments based on market conditions and performance. Stay flexible and be willing to make changes to your strategy to manage risks and achieve your investment goals.

Diversification and Hedging Techniques
Diversification and hedging are essential strategies for managing risk and enhancing the potential for profits. By spreading your investments across different sectors and using hedging techniques, you can protect your portfolio and achieve consistent returns.

Diversification Strategies

Diversification is a fundamental principle of risk management in investment. By spreading investments across different sectors, geographical regions, asset classes, and market capitalizations, investors can reduce the impact of adverse events on their portfolios and enhance long-term returns. Let's explore various diversification strategies in more detail:

Sector Diversification
Benefits:
Diversifying across sectors helps mitigate risks associated with sector-specific events or economic downturns. Different sectors perform differently under various market conditions, so spreading investments across sectors can balance portfolio performance.

Example:
Suppose an investor allocates funds to technology, healthcare, and consumer staples sectors. If the technology sector experiences a downturn due to regulatory changes, the

investor's exposure to healthcare and consumer staples sectors can offset potential losses.

Geographical Diversification
Benefits:
Investing in stocks from different geographical regions helps reduce risks associated with country-specific events, political instability, or economic downturns. It also provides exposure to diverse economies, currencies, and market cycles.

Example:
An investor diversifies their portfolio by allocating funds to stocks from the United States, Europe, Asia-Pacific, and emerging markets. If one region experiences a recession or geopolitical turmoil, the investor's exposure to other regions can cushion the impact on their portfolio.

Asset Class Diversification
Benefits:

Including various asset classes in a portfolio provides additional diversification benefits. Different asset classes, such as stocks, bonds, real estate, and commodities, have unique risk-return profiles and tend to perform differently under different market conditions.

Example:
An investor diversifies their portfolio by allocating funds to stocks, bonds, and real estate investment trusts (REITs). During periods of stock market volatility, the fixed-income component of bonds can provide stability and income, while REITs offer exposure to the real estate market.

Market Capitalization Diversification
Benefits:
Investing in stocks with different market capitalizations—large-cap, mid-cap, and small-cap—balances the stability of established companies with the growth potential of smaller firms. Large-cap stocks are typically more stable

but offer lower growth potential, while small-cap stocks are more volatile but offer higher growth prospects.

Example:
An investor diversifies their portfolio by allocating funds to a mix of large-cap, mid-cap, and small-cap stocks. Large-cap stocks provide stability during market downturns, while mid-cap and small-cap stocks offer potential for higher returns during periods of economic expansion.

Practical Tips for Diversification
Regular Portfolio Reviews:
Conduct periodic reviews of your portfolio to ensure it remains diversified according to your investment goals and risk tolerance. Rebalance your portfolio as needed to maintain proper diversification.

Stay Informed:

Stay updated on market developments, economic indicators, and industry trends that may affect your diversified portfolio. Being informed allows you to make informed decisions about rebalancing or adjusting your allocations.

Consider Global Events:
Pay attention to global events, such as geopolitical tensions, economic policy changes, or natural disasters, that may impact different sectors or regions of the world. Adjust your diversification strategy accordingly to mitigate risks.

Consult Financial Advisors:
Seek guidance from financial advisors or investment professionals when designing your diversification strategy. They can provide personalized recommendations based on your financial situation, goals, and risk tolerance.

By implementing these diversification strategies, investors can build resilient portfolios that can weather market volatility and achieve long-term financial objectives. Diversification is not only about spreading risk but also about capturing opportunities for growth across different sectors and asset classes.

Chapter 5: Executing Sympathy Plays

Executing sympathy plays requires a combination of strategic planning, timely execution, and disciplined risk management. This chapter will guide you through the process of executing sympathy plays effectively, including identifying entry and exit points, timing your trades, setting realistic targets and stop-losses, monitoring and adjusting your positions, and making necessary adjustments to your strategy.

Entry and Exit Points
Identifying Entry Points:
Entry points are critical in sympathy plays, as they determine when you initiate a trade to capitalize on potential price movements. Look for specific catalysts or triggers that signal an

opportunity for a sympathy play. These catalysts could include positive news announcements, earnings reports, or technical indicators.

Examples of Entry Points:

Positive news from a leading company in a sector may trigger sympathy moves in related stocks.
Breakout patterns on technical charts indicating bullish momentum.
Options activity indicating bullish sentiment or unusual volume.
Setting Exit Points:
Exit points are equally important and help you lock in profits or minimize losses. Define clear exit criteria based on your trading strategy and risk tolerance. This could include setting profit targets, trailing stop-loss orders, or predefined technical levels.

Examples of Exit Points:

Achieving a predetermined profit target based on your trading plan.

The stock reaching a technical resistance level, signaling potential price reversal.

Trailing stop-loss orders triggered by adverse price movements to protect against losses.

Timing Your Trades

Understanding Market Dynamics:

Timing plays a crucial role in executing sympathy plays successfully. Pay attention to market dynamics, including trading volume, liquidity, and volatility levels. These factors influence the timing of your trades and the likelihood of achieving your desired outcomes.

Considerations for Timing:

Market Open: Price movements are often more volatile during the opening minutes of trading. Consider entering trades shortly after the market open to capitalize on initial momentum.

Earnings Releases: Trading around earnings announcements can be lucrative but also risky.

Consider waiting until after earnings releases to assess market reactions before entering trades.
Intraday Trends: Monitor intraday trends and volume patterns to identify optimal entry and exit points. Adjust your timing based on evolving market conditions throughout the trading day.

Setting Realistic Targets and Stop-Losses

Establishing Profit Targets:

Profit targets help you define your desired outcomes and manage your expectations. Set realistic profit targets based on your trading strategy, risk-reward ratio, and market conditions. Consider factors such as historical price movements, technical analysis, and sector trends when setting profit targets.

Implementing Stop-Loss Orders:

Stop-loss orders are essential risk management tools that help protect your capital from significant losses. Place stop-loss orders at predefined price levels to limit potential downside risk. Adjust stop-loss levels based on changes in market conditions, but ensure they align with your risk tolerance and trading plan.

Monitoring and Adjusting

Continuous Monitoring:
Stay vigilant and monitor your positions regularly to assess their performance and evaluate market conditions. Keep track of news developments, economic indicators, and technical signals that may impact your trades. Use trading platforms, financial news sources, and real-time data to stay informed.

Making Necessary Adjustments:
Be prepared to make adjustments to your positions and trading strategy as needed. If market conditions change or new information emerges, reassess your trades and consider whether adjustments are warranted. This could involve scaling into or out of positions, adjusting stop-loss levels, or closing trades prematurely.

Keeping Track of Market Conditions

Stay Informed:
Stay updated on market conditions, sector trends, and macroeconomic factors that may affect your trades. Regularly review financial news, industry reports, and economic data releases to gauge market sentiment and identify potential opportunities or risks.

Technical Analysis:
Utilize technical analysis tools and indicators to analyze price patterns, trends, and support/resistance levels. Technical analysis can help you identify optimal entry and exit points, as well as gauge the strength of market trends.

Fundamental Analysis:
Conduct fundamental analysis to assess the underlying value and growth prospects of the stocks you're trading. Evaluate factors such as earnings growth, revenue projections, and competitive positioning to make informed trading decisions.

Making Necessary Adjustments to Your Strategy
Adaptability:
Be flexible and adaptable in your approach to trading sympathy plays. Market conditions can change rapidly, requiring you to adjust your strategy accordingly. Stay open to new information and be willing to pivot if your original thesis no longer holds true.

Learn from Experience:
Review your trading results and learn from both successes and failures. Identify patterns and trends in your trading performance and use this information to refine your strategy over time. Continuous improvement is key to long-term success in trading.

Risk Management:
Prioritize risk management at all times. Protecting your capital should be your primary focus, and this requires discipline and adherence to your trading plan. Avoid taking excessive risks

or chasing speculative opportunities that could jeopardize your financial stability.

Conclusion

Executing sympathy plays requires a combination of strategic planning, market awareness, and disciplined execution. By identifying entry and exit points, timing your trades effectively, setting realistic targets and stop-losses, monitoring market conditions, and making necessary adjustments to your strategy, you can enhance your chances of success in trading sympathy plays. Remember to stay informed, stay disciplined, and prioritize risk management to achieve consistent results over time.

Chapter 6: Common Pitfalls and How to Avoid Them

Trading sympathy plays can be lucrative, but it also comes with its share of challenges and pitfalls. In this chapter, we'll explore common mistakes and errors in sympathy trading, how to recognize and correct them, the importance of learning from failures, and strategies for building resilience and adaptability.

Mistakes to Avoid

1. Overtrading:

Overtrading occurs when traders execute too many trades, often in quick succession, without proper analysis or justification. This can lead to increased transaction costs, emotional exhaustion, and impulsive decision-making.

2. Chasing Momentum:

Chasing momentum involves entering trades based solely on recent price movements without considering underlying fundamentals or technical indicators. While momentum trading can be profitable, it's essential to distinguish between sustainable trends and short-lived spikes.

3. Ignoring Risk Management:
Neglecting risk management is a common pitfall that can result in significant losses. Traders may fail to set stop-loss orders, ignore position sizing principles, or disregard overall portfolio risk. Proper risk management is crucial for preserving capital and long-term success.

4. Lack of Discipline:
Lack of discipline manifests in various forms, such as deviating from trading plans, succumbing to emotional impulses, or failing to adhere to predetermined rules. Discipline is essential for maintaining consistency and avoiding costly mistakes.

5. Failing to Adapt:
Market conditions are dynamic and constantly evolving. Failing to adapt to changing circumstances, such as shifts in sentiment, economic indicators, or sector trends, can result in missed opportunities or losses.

Common Errors in Sympathy Trading
1. Blindly Following the Crowd:
Many traders fall into the trap of blindly following the crowd or herd mentality. They may rush to buy or sell stocks based on popular sentiment or social media hype without conducting thorough analysis. This can lead to herd-driven price bubbles or panics.

2. Overlooking Individual Stock Factors:
While sympathy plays are based on the premise of related stocks moving in tandem, it's essential to consider individual stock factors. Each company has unique fundamentals, competitive

positioning, and growth prospects that may diverge from sector trends.

3. Failing to Research Catalysts:
Successful sympathy trading requires identifying and understanding catalysts that drive price movements. Failing to research and assess these catalysts can result in missed opportunities or unexpected losses.

4. Neglecting Technical Analysis:
Technical analysis provides valuable insights into price patterns, trends, and support/resistance levels. Neglecting technical analysis or relying solely on fundamental analysis can lead to suboptimal trading decisions.

5. Emotional Decision-Making:
Emotions such as fear, greed, and FOMO (fear of missing out) can cloud judgment and lead to irrational decision-making. Traders may panic sell during market downturns or chase

speculative stocks based on hype, resulting in losses.

How to Recognize and Correct Them

1. Maintain a Trading Journal:
Keep a detailed trading journal to record your trades, including entry and exit points, rationale, and outcomes. Reviewing your journal regularly can help you identify recurring mistakes and patterns, allowing you to take corrective action.

2. Stick to Your Trading Plan:
Develop a well-defined trading plan that outlines your objectives, strategies, risk tolerance, and rules for entering and exiting trades. Stick to your plan religiously and avoid deviating from it based on emotions or impulsive decisions.

3. Practice Patience and Discipline:
Exercise patience and discipline in your trading approach. Avoid rushing into trades or making impulsive decisions based on short-term

fluctuations. Take the time to conduct thorough analysis and wait for optimal entry points.

4. Incorporate Risk Management:
Prioritize risk management in your trading strategy. Set appropriate stop-loss orders, manage position sizes to limit exposure, and diversify your portfolio to spread risk. Implementing robust risk management practices can help protect your capital and minimize losses.

5. Continuously Educate Yourself:
Stay informed about market developments, trading strategies, and psychological aspects of trading. Continuously educate yourself through books, courses, webinars, and mentorship programs. The more knowledgeable you are, the better equipped you'll be to navigate the markets effectively.

Learning from Failures
1. Analyze Your Mistakes:

When faced with losses or setbacks, take the time to analyze your mistakes objectively. Identify the root causes of your failures, whether they're related to strategy, execution, or mindset.

2. Extract Lessons Learned:
Extract valuable lessons from your failures and use them to improve your trading approach. Determine what went wrong, what could have been done differently, and how you can avoid similar mistakes in the future.

3. Embrace Failure as a Learning Opportunity:
View failure as a natural part of the learning process rather than a setback. Embrace failure as an opportunity to grow, adapt, and become a better trader. Every mistake presents a chance to refine your skills and strategies.

4. Maintain a Growth Mindset:
Cultivate a growth mindset that focuses on continuous learning and improvement. Embrace challenges, seek feedback, and remain resilient

in the face of adversity. Remember that successful traders are not defined by their failures but by their ability to bounce back and persevere.

Turning Mistakes into Learning Opportunities

1. Adjust Your Trading Plan:
Based on your analysis of past mistakes, make necessary adjustments to your trading plan. Modify your strategies, rules, or risk management techniques to address areas of weakness and improve your chances of success.

2. Practice Risk-Aware Trading:
Shift your focus from chasing profits to managing risks effectively. Prioritize capital preservation and focus on minimizing losses rather than maximizing gains. Implementing risk-aware trading practices can lead to more consistent and sustainable results over time.

3. Seek Feedback and Mentorship:

Seek feedback from experienced traders or mentors who can provide valuable insights and guidance. Learn from their experiences, mistakes, and successes, and apply those lessons to your own trading journey.

4. Stay Resilient and Persistent:
Trading is inherently challenging, and setbacks are inevitable. Stay resilient and persistent in pursuing your trading goals despite obstacles or failures. Use setbacks as fuel to propel you forward and continue striving for improvement.

Building Resilience and Adaptability
1. Cultivate Emotional Intelligence:
Develop emotional intelligence skills to better manage stress, anxiety, and fear in trading. Practice mindfulness techniques, such as deep breathing or visualization, to stay calm and focused during volatile market conditions.

2. Stay Flexible and Adaptive:

Remain flexible and adaptive in your trading approach. Be open to new ideas, strategies, and opportunities that may arise. Adapt to changing market conditions and be willing to adjust your tactics accordingly.

3. Focus on Long-Term Growth:
Shift your mindset from short-term gains to long-term growth and sustainability. Set realistic expectations, prioritize consistency over high-risk gambles, and focus on building a solid foundation for your trading career.

4. Learn from Every Experience:
Approach trading as a continuous learning journey. Extract insights from every trade, whether it's a success or a failure, and use those experiences to refine your skills, strategies, and mindset.

By recognizing common pitfalls, learning from mistakes, and cultivating resilience and adaptability, you can navigate the challenges of sympathy trading more effectively and increase your chances of success in the markets. Remember that trading is a marathon, not a sprint.

Chapter 7: Advanced Techniques and Insights

In this chapter, we look at advanced techniques and insights for maximizing your success in sympathy trading. We'll explore how to leverage technology and tools effectively, utilize financial software and analytics, automate trading processes with algorithmic strategies, integrate sympathy plays into your broader investment strategy, and balance short-term trades with long-term investment approaches.

Leveraging Technology and Tools
1. Real-Time Market Data:
Access to real-time market data is essential for making informed trading decisions. Utilize financial platforms and data providers that offer up-to-date information on stock prices, volume, news, and technical indicators.

2. Trading Platforms:
Choose a reliable trading platform that suits your trading style and preferences. Look for platforms with advanced charting tools, customizable layouts, and fast execution speeds. Popular platforms include thinkorswim, MetaTrader, and Interactive Brokers.

3. Stock Screeners:
Utilize stock screeners to filter stocks based on specific criteria such as sector, industry, market capitalization, and technical indicators. Stock screeners help you identify potential sympathy plays and streamline your research process.

4. Technical Analysis Software:
Invest in technical analysis software that offers advanced charting capabilities, technical indicators, and pattern recognition tools. Platforms like TradingView, StockCharts, and TC2000 provide robust features for analyzing price movements and identifying trading opportunities.

Using Financial Software and Analytics

1. Fundamental Analysis Tools:

Utilize fundamental analysis tools to assess the financial health and growth prospects of companies. Look for software that offers comprehensive financial data, earnings reports, and valuation metrics to inform your investment decisions.

2. Economic Data Platforms:

Stay informed about macroeconomic trends and indicators using economic data platforms. Access key economic indicators, central bank announcements, and geopolitical events that may impact market sentiment and sector performance.

3. Sentiment Analysis Tools:

Monitor market sentiment and social media chatter using sentiment analysis tools. These tools analyze news articles, social media posts, and online discussions to gauge investor sentiment and identify emerging trends or sentiment shifts.

Automation and Algorithmic Trading

1. Algorithmic Trading Strategies:
Explore algorithmic trading strategies that leverage automated processes and predefined rules to execute trades. Develop algorithms based on technical indicators, statistical models, or machine learning algorithms to capitalize on sympathy plays and market inefficiencies.

2. Backtesting and Optimization:
Backtest and optimize your algorithmic trading strategies using historical data to assess their performance and refine their parameters. Use backtesting platforms and simulation tools to evaluate different strategies and identify optimal settings.

3. Execution Algorithms:
Utilize execution algorithms to optimize trade execution and minimize market impact.

Execution algorithms, such as VWAP (Volume-Weighted Average Price) and TWAP (Time-Weighted Average Price), help traders execute large orders efficiently without disrupting the market.

Integrating Sympathy Plays into Your Broader Investment Strategy

1. Portfolio Allocation:
Integrate sympathy plays into your broader investment portfolio by allocating a portion of your capital to sector-specific opportunities. Diversify your portfolio across different sectors and asset classes to spread risk and capture opportunities for growth.

2. Risk Management:
Incorporate sympathy plays into your risk management framework by setting clear risk parameters and diversifying your trades. Manage position sizes, set stop-loss orders, and monitor overall portfolio risk to protect your capital and minimize losses.

3. Long-Term Investment Thesis:
Align sympathy plays with your long-term investment thesis and strategic goals. Consider how sector trends, regulatory changes, and technological advancements may influence the long-term prospects of related stocks and industries.

Balancing Sympathy Trades with Other Investment Approaches

1. Scalability and Liquidity:
Consider the scalability and liquidity of sympathy trades relative to other investment approaches. While sympathy plays offer short-term trading opportunities, long-term investment strategies may provide more stable returns and liquidity for larger positions.

2. Risk-Reward Profile:
Evaluate the risk-reward profile of sympathy trades compared to other investment approaches. Balance the potential for short-term

gains in sympathy trading with the stability and growth potential of long-term investments.

3. Diversification Benefits:
Assess the diversification benefits of incorporating sympathy trades into your overall investment strategy. Sympathy plays can complement other investment approaches by providing exposure to different sectors, market trends, and trading opportunities.

Long-Term vs. Short-Term Strategies
1. Short-Term Trading Tactics:
Short-term trading tactics focus on capitalizing on immediate price movements and market inefficiencies. Sympathy plays are well-suited for short-term trading strategies due to their reactive nature and potential for rapid price changes.

2. Long-Term Investment Horizon:
Long-term investment strategies take a broader view of market trends and fundamental factors.

While sympathy plays can offer short-term trading opportunities, long-term investors may prioritize fundamentals, growth prospects, and dividend income for sustainable wealth creation.

3. Hybrid Approaches:
Consider hybrid approaches that blend elements of both short-term trading and long-term investing. This may involve using sympathy plays to generate short-term profits while maintaining core positions in high-quality stocks for long-term growth and stability.

Conclusion
Advanced techniques and insights can enhance your proficiency in sympathy trading and elevate your overall investment strategy. By leveraging technology, utilizing financial software and analytics, automating trading processes, integrating sympathy plays into your broader investment strategy, balancing short-term trades with long-term approaches, and understanding the nuances of different trading tactics, you can

optimize your trading performance and achieve your financial goals. Remember to stay informed, remain adaptable, and continuously refine your skills to stay ahead in the ever-evolving world of finance.

Chapter 8: Building a Community and Continuous Learning

In the dynamic world of investing, building a supportive community and fostering a culture of continuous learning are essential for long-term success. In this chapter, we'll explore the importance of engaging with other investors, joining investment groups and forums, sharing insights and strategies, staying informed about market news and trends, and prioritizing continuous learning and improvement.

Engaging with Other Investors
1. Networking Opportunities:
Engaging with other investors provides valuable networking opportunities to exchange ideas, share experiences, and learn from each other's successes and failures. Join investment clubs,

attend conferences, and participate in networking events to connect with like-minded individuals.

2. Peer Support and Encouragement:
Building a community of fellow investors offers peer support and encouragement during both challenging times and triumphs. Surround yourself with individuals who share your passion for investing and can offer valuable insights and advice along your journey.

3. Diverse Perspectives:
Interacting with investors from diverse backgrounds and expertise areas exposes you to different perspectives and investment strategies. Embrace diversity in thought and approach, and be open to learning from investors with varying experiences and viewpoints.

Joining Investment Groups and Forums
1. Online Communities:

Join online investment groups and forums to connect with a broader community of investors worldwide. Platforms like Reddit, StockTwits, and Seeking Alpha host active communities where members discuss market trends, share research, and exchange trading ideas.

2. Specialized Forums:
Explore specialized forums and discussion groups focused on specific investment themes, sectors, or trading strategies. These forums provide targeted insights and discussions tailored to your interests and objectives, allowing you to deepen your knowledge in niche areas.

3. Local Meetups:
Participate in local investment meetups or user groups to connect with investors in your area. These gatherings offer opportunities for face-to-face interactions, networking, and knowledge sharing within your local investing community.

Sharing Insights and Strategies

1. Contributing to Discussions:

Contribute actively to investment discussions by sharing your insights, analysis, and trading strategies. Engage in thoughtful dialogue with fellow investors, ask questions, and provide constructive feedback to enhance the collective learning experience.

2. Blogging and Content Creation:

Consider blogging or creating content to share your investment journey, research findings, and trading experiences. Publishing articles, podcasts, or videos allows you to reach a wider audience and establish yourself as a thought leader in your area of expertise.

3. Mentorship and Coaching:

Offer mentorship and coaching to less experienced investors seeking guidance and support. Sharing your knowledge and expertise not only benefits others but also reinforces your own understanding and mastery of investment concepts.

Staying Informed

1. Market News and Updates:
Stay informed about market news, economic indicators, and geopolitical events that may impact your investments. Follow reputable financial news sources, subscribe to newsletters, and set up alerts to receive timely updates on relevant developments.

2. Sector Research and Analysis:
Conduct thorough research and analysis on sectors and industries of interest to identify emerging trends, opportunities, and risks. Stay abreast of sector-specific news, earnings reports, and regulatory developments to inform your investment decisions.

3. Technical and Fundamental Analysis:
Stay updated on advances in technical and fundamental analysis techniques to enhance

your trading skills. Continuously refine your ability to analyze price charts, interpret financial statements, and assess company fundamentals to make informed investment decisions.

Keeping Up with Market News and Trends
1. Follow Industry Leaders:
Follow industry leaders, analysts, and influencers on social media platforms, blogs, and podcasts to gain insights into market trends and investment strategies. Pay attention to their commentary, recommendations, and market outlooks to inform your own decisions.

2. Attend Webinars and Workshops:
Participate in webinars, workshops, and online seminars hosted by reputable organizations and industry experts. These educational sessions cover a wide range of topics, from technical analysis techniques to macroeconomic trends, providing valuable insights and learning opportunities.

3. Read Books and Research Reports:
Read books, research reports, and academic papers to deepen your understanding of investment concepts and methodologies. Explore both classic texts and contemporary literature to gain diverse perspectives and insights into various investment approaches.

Continuous Learning and Improvement

1. Set Learning Goals:
Set specific learning goals and objectives to guide your continuous learning journey. Identify areas for improvement, such as technical analysis skills, fundamental analysis knowledge, or risk management techniques, and develop a plan to enhance your proficiency in those areas.

2. Commit to Lifelong Learning:
Embrace a mindset of lifelong learning and commitment to continuous improvement in your investment practice. Stay curious, seek out new opportunities for learning, and remain open to

acquiring new skills and knowledge throughout your investing career.

3. Reflect and Iterate:
Regularly reflect on your investment decisions, trading outcomes, and learning experiences to identify areas for growth and refinement. Iterate on your strategies, techniques, and processes based on lessons learned and feedback received to continually elevate your performance.

Conclusion
Building a community of fellow investors and fostering a culture of continuous learning are foundational elements of success in the world of investing. By engaging with other investors, joining investment groups and forums, sharing insights and strategies, staying informed about market news and trends, and prioritizing continuous learning and improvement, you can enhance your knowledge, skills, and confidence as an investor. Embrace the journey of lifelong learning, connect with a supportive community,

and strive for excellence in your investment practice.

Conclusion:

In this comprehensive guide, we've explored the fascinating world of sympathy trading, uncovering its potential for generating profits in the stock market. From understanding the phenomenon of sympathy moves to executing strategic trades and navigating common pitfalls, we've covered a wide range of topics to equip you with the knowledge and tools needed to succeed as a sympathy trader. As we conclude our journey, let's recap the key points, summarize the main takeaways, offer final thoughts and encouragement, and discuss next steps for implementing what you've learned.

Recap of Key Points
Understanding Sympathy Moves: Sympathy moves occur when the price of one stock influences the price of related stocks in the same sector or industry. By identifying these

relationships and catalysts, traders can capitalize on price movements for potential profits.

Executing Sympathy Plays: Successfully executing sympathy plays requires strategic planning, timing, and risk management. From identifying entry and exit points to setting realistic targets and stop-losses, traders must navigate the intricacies of the market with discipline and precision.

Risk Management: Prioritizing risk management is paramount in sympathy trading to protect capital and minimize losses. Implementing stop-loss orders, diversifying portfolios, and adhering to trading plans are essential practices for mitigating risk.

Continuous Learning: The journey of becoming a successful trader is one of continuous learning and improvement. Engaging with other investors, staying informed about market news and trends, and refining trading strategies are crucial aspects of ongoing education in the dynamic world of investing.

Summarizing the Main Takeaways

Community and Collaboration: Building a community of fellow investors and engaging in meaningful dialogue fosters learning, growth, and support. Share insights, exchange ideas, and collaborate with others to enhance your trading journey.

Adaptability and Resilience: The ability to adapt to changing market conditions and bounce back from setbacks is essential for long-term success in trading. Cultivate resilience, embrace challenges, and remain flexible in your approach.

Continuous Improvement: Commit to a mindset of continuous improvement and lifelong learning. Reflect on your experiences, iterate on your strategies, and seek out opportunities for growth and development as an investor.

Final Thoughts and Encouragement

As you embark on your journey as a sympathy trader, remember that success in the market is not guaranteed, and setbacks are inevitable. However, with dedication, perseverance, and a willingness to learn, you can navigate the complexities of trading and achieve your financial goals. Embrace the journey with optimism, resilience, and a thirst for knowledge, and trust in your ability to adapt and thrive in the ever-evolving world of finance.

Next Steps

Now that you've gained a solid understanding of sympathy trading and acquired valuable insights and strategies, it's time to take action. Here are some next steps to start implementing what you've learned:

Practice Patience and Discipline: Approach trading with patience, discipline, and a long-term perspective. Avoid impulsive decisions and stick to your trading plan with unwavering commitment.

Start Small and Gradually Scale Up: Begin with small trades to test your strategies and build confidence. As you gain experience and success, gradually increase position sizes and scale up your trading activity.

Keep Learning and Adapting: Stay curious, stay informed, and stay adaptable. Continuously seek out opportunities for learning, refine your skills, and adapt your strategies based on evolving market conditions.

Seek Feedback and Mentorship: Don't hesitate to seek feedback from experienced traders or mentors who can offer guidance and support. Learn from their experiences, leverage their insights, and incorporate their advice into your trading approach.

Stay Resilient and Persistent: Trading can be challenging and unpredictable, but don't let setbacks deter you. Stay resilient in the face of adversity, learn from failures, and keep pushing forward with determination and perseverance.

By taking these steps and implementing the knowledge and strategies you've acquired, you'll be well-positioned to embark on a successful journey as a sympathy trader. Embrace the opportunities, embrace the challenges, and embrace the journey with enthusiasm and determination. Here's to your success in the exciting world of sympathy trading!

Bonus Template and Checklist

Strategy Development Template

1. Define Your Objectives
Clearly articulate your financial goals and objectives for trading.
Specify your target returns, risk tolerance, and time horizon.

2. Assess Market Conditions
Analyze current market trends, sector performance, and macroeconomic factors.
Identify potential catalysts or triggers that may influence market movements.

3. Research Sympathy Plays
Identify sectors or industries with strong correlations and interdependencies.

Conduct thorough research on related stocks, including their fundamentals, recent news, and historical price movements.

4. Set Entry and Exit Criteria

Define specific entry and exit points for your trades based on technical and/or fundamental analysis.
Establish criteria for identifying favorable trade setups and determining when to exit positions.

5. Develop Risk Management Plan

Determine your maximum risk per trade and overall portfolio risk limits.
Implement risk management techniques such as stop-loss orders, position sizing, and diversification.

6. Test and Refine Your Strategy

Backtest your strategy using historical data to assess its performance.
Identify strengths and weaknesses, and make necessary adjustments to optimize your strategy.

7. Monitor and Evaluate

Continuously monitor market conditions and track the performance of your trades.

Evaluate the effectiveness of your strategy and make adjustments as needed to adapt to changing market dynamics.

Risk Management Checklist

1. Position Sizing

Determine the appropriate position size for each trade based on your risk tolerance and account size.

Avoid overcommitting capital to any single trade, and adhere to predetermined position sizing rules.

2. Stop-Loss Orders

Always use stop-loss orders to limit potential losses and protect capital.

Set stop-loss levels based on technical support/resistance levels, volatility, and your risk management plan.

3. Portfolio Diversification

Diversify your portfolio across different sectors, asset classes, and trading strategies.

Avoid overconcentration in any single stock or sector to reduce portfolio risk.

4. Risk-Reward Ratio

Assess the risk-reward ratio for each trade to ensure that potential rewards outweigh potential losses.

Aim for a minimum risk-reward ratio of 1:2 or higher to justify trades and maintain a positive expectancy.

5. Review and Adjust

Regularly review your risk management plan and trading performance to identify areas for improvement.

Adjust your risk management techniques as needed based on changes in market conditions or trading objectives.

6. Emotional Discipline

Maintain emotional discipline and avoid making impulsive decisions based on fear or greed.
Stick to your risk management plan and trading rules, even during periods of market volatility or uncertainty.

7. Contingency Planning
Develop contingency plans for unexpected events or adverse market conditions.
Consider potential scenarios and have predefined strategies in place to mitigate risks and protect capital.

8. Continuous Learning
Stay informed about risk management best practices and market developments.
Continuously educate yourself and adapt your risk management techniques to evolving market conditions and trading environments.
By following these templates and checklists, you can develop a robust trading strategy and implement effective risk management practices to navigate the challenges of the market

successfully. Remember to remain disciplined, stay vigilant, and prioritize the preservation of capital in your trading endeavors.

Harmony Weaver

www.ingramcontent.com/pod-product-compliance
Lightning Source LLC
Chambersburg PA
CBHW070248230526
45470CB00002B/525